WINGATE'S MEN

The Chindit Operations: Special Forces in Burma

WINGATE'S MEN

The Chindit Operations: Special Forces in Burma

COLIN HIGGS

FRONTLINE
BOOKS

Wingate's Men
The Chindit Operations: Special Forces in Burma

First published in Great Britain in 2019 by
Frontline Books
An imprint of
Pen & Sword Books Ltd
Yorkshire - Philadelphia

ISBN 978 1 52674 667 2

A CIP catalogue record for this book is
available from the British Library

Typeset in 10/13 pt Palatino
by Aura Technology and Software Services, India

Printed and bound by CPI Group (UK) Ltd, Croydon, CR0 4YY

Pen & Sword Books Ltd incorporates the Imprints of Aviation, Atlas,
Family History, Fiction, Maritime, Military, Discovery, Politics, History,
Archaeology, Select, Wharncliffe Local History, Wharncliffe True Crime,
Military Classics, Wharncliffe Transport, Leo Cooper, The Praetorian Press,
Remember When, Seaforth Publishing and Frontline Publishing.

For a complete list of Pen & Sword titles please contact

PEN & SWORD BOOKS LTD
47 Church Street, Barnsley, South Yorkshire, S70 2AS, England
E-mail: enquiries@pen-and-sword.co.uk
Website: www.pen-and-sword.co.uk

Or

PEN AND SWORD BOOKS
1950 Lawrence Rd, Havertown, PA 19083, USA
E-mail: Uspen-and-sword@casematepublishers.com
Website: www.penandswordbooks.com

Contents

Introduction

MY DAD WAS a talker. He liked nothing better than to sit down of an evening, with a whisky by his side, and talk about his two favourite subjects, the British Army and cricket. But through all those long evenings he spent very little time talking about his exploits in India and Burma during the Second World War unless, that is, he was talking about playing cricket for the Army, the Indian Army and even the Punjab.

My Dad went out to India in 1943. In August of that year he took part in a convoy from Lahore to Meshed, now Mashhad, in Iran as part of a Motor Ambulance Section of the Royal Indian Army Service Corps, the task being to take maintenance spares and return with American stores for China. That was a distance of over 2,000 miles each way.

That I know as I have photographs and they were times he talked about. What remained unspoken was his journey with the Gurkhas on Orde Wingate's second Chindit expedition from March 1944. I have his slouch hat; I have his kukri; and I have his Chindit shoulder badge which were carried or worn by him on the expedition, but whenever I asked him for some detail he would just smile and say nothing apart from referring to the still recurring bouts of malaria. No doubt there had been something that stopped him from speaking about it.

The Chindits were a multi-national force involving units from Britain and her allies, including the Gurkhas, Nigerian regiments, volunteers from Hong Kong, men of the Burma Rifles and a huge support group provided by both the RAF and the USAAF. On the ground with the soldiers went signals and forward air controllers. The expedition involved a massive logistics campaign supplying everything required from the air. Those involved on the ground had to battle against not only the Japanese but also the intense Burmese heat, the ravages of dysentery and malaria and constant movement carrying heavy permanently-wet packs which caused awful jungle sores that should have required hospitalisation.

Almost seventy-five years later just a few of the Chindits are left to tell their stories. My Dad passed away in 1991 having been persuaded by his father to leave the forces in 1946 and join the bank as he was told that 'there was no future in the army', a decision he regretted for the rest of his life. He joined the Territorials, rose to command 160 Regiment RCT

and ended his days as President of Surrey's British Legion. But he was just one of the reasons why I wanted to compile this book.

This is not a history of the Chindit operations although a brief history is included. This is a tribute not only to all the Chindits who trekked, and fought, through appalling terrain on both expeditions but to all the soldiers, sailors and airmen who fought in that most inhospitable of battlefields throughout the war with Japan.

Colin Higgs,
Dorset, 2019

'MARCH DIVIDED BUT FIGHT UNITED'

IT IS STATED that the Chindits were the largest of the Allied Special Forces organisations of the Second World War. Formed and lead by Major General Orde Wingate DSO & Two Bars, at least until his death in March 1944, the Chindits operated in the dense jungles of Burma.

It would be impossible in the space permitted here to explore their story in great detail. Instead, we will use the words of Lieutenant Colonel Frank Owen OBE who, in 1946, was tasked by the Central Office of Information to provide a concise account of the Burma Campaign for South-East Asia Command. It is the three chapters that Lieutenant Colonel Owen wrote on the Chindits that follow and which we have kept, as far as is possible, faithful to his original writing.

WINGATE'S FIRST MISSION

THE LATE MAJOR-GENERAL Orde Charles Wingate, DSO, was an unusual man. He commanded the confidence of unusual men, too. Wavell believed in him, and twice already had given him his head – in Palestine before the war, where he had organised a Jewish volunteer militia to fight Arab terrorism, and in Abyssinia in 1940-41, when he had proved his guerrilla genius as a leader of the patriots against the Italians. Later, Churchill would find himself in harmony with his daring and powerful mind. Mountbatten, too, in the days to come would take this strange man to his heart, encourage him and back him to the limit, even when he was being temperamental.

Wingate was one who did not joyfully suffer opposition. He drew down the lightning on his own head, alas, in the final, tragic sense, for he was killed in his hour of triumph, flying with characteristic defiance through an electric storm. When he fell, his friend and Commanding Officer, Lieutenant-General William Slim, Commander of Fourteenth Army, wrote a tribute to him in which he analysed his quality as leader. 'Wingate had clear vision,' wrote Slim. 'He could also impart his belief to others. Above all, he could adapt to his own purpose the ideas, practices and techniques of others once he was satisfied of their soundness. To see Wingate urging action on some hesitant commander was to realise how a medieval baron felt when Peter the Hermit got after him to go crusading. Lots of barons found Peter the Hermit an uncomfortable fellow, but they went crusading all the same.'

Field Marshal Wavell inspecting the men of the Chindits in February 1943, before the start of the first march into Burma.

Wingate himself considered that 'the chief difference between a good and bad commander is an accurate imagination'.

Early in 1942, during the retreat from Burma, Wavell had applied for his services to organise guerrilla levies. By the time he arrived the campaign was almost over. Wingate drew from it the necessary deductions and set before Wavell a plan to carry Japanese envelopment tactics a stage beyond their own practice. He proposed a specially trained and organised brigade, which should penetrate deep into enemy territory and operate there by means of air supply and wireless without depending on the normal military lines of communication. 'The vulnerable artery is the Line of Communication winding through the jungle,' said Wingate. 'Have no L. of C. on the jungle floor. Bring in the goods, like Father Christmas, down the chimney."

Wavell approved. A formation was created, to be known as the 77th Indian Infantry Brigade comprising the 13th Battalion, King's Liverpool Regiment, 3rd/2nd Gurkha Rifles 2nd Battalion Burma Rifles, and the 142nd Commando Company. These units were in no sense hand-picked: they were those which were available. They were placed under Wingate's command, and in July 1942 were moved to the Central Provinces to begin an intensive course of jungle training, based on Wingate's own experience and theories.

Wavell had schemed that Wingate's Brigade should cut enemy communications south of Myitkyina – the capital city of Kachin State and some 900 miles north of Yangon (formerly known as Rangoon) – as Stilwell advanced into North Burma. But early in February 1943 it became plain that there would be no Chinese offensive from Yunnan.

As the prospect of a joint campaign vanished, Wavell had to consider whether or not he should employ the brigade at all. It had concentrated at Imphal in seven self-contained columns, marching down from railhead at Dimapur 120 miles away.

On the evening of 6 February, Wavell held a long conference with Wingate and decided to let him go on with his expedition alone. Next morning, he inspected the force and watched as the men marched off towards Tamu, bound for Burma. Hundreds of pack-mules, oxen and even elephants accompanied them. The RAF, however, was to provide the main supply system of the expedition, so air liaison officers were attached to each column and on its march towards the frontier Wingate's brigade practised close co-operation with the 'planes.

The brigade's directive was to enter the country through the front held by the IVth Corps, to cut the main railway line between Mandalay and Myitkyina, harass the enemy in the Shwebo area, and finally, if Wingate considered the conditions favourable, to cross the Irrawaddy and cut the railway between Mandalay and Lashio. It was vital to conceal these intentions from the enemy and to get beyond the Chindwin River to the Mandalay-Myitkyina railway, 150 miles to the east, without being detected.

As deception, a couple of Gurkha columns crossed the Chindwin three days ahead of the main body and fifty miles to the south. Already, the 23rd Indian Division was simulating an attack on Kalewa, and the Gurkha decoy force created the additional demonstration required for the rest of the brigade to pass over the Chindwin undisturbed. These main forces advanced rapidly towards the railway, which they reached after a fortnight's march through deep jungle – and not without fighting. The RAF air-drop supply system came through this first important test with almost 100 per cent success.

It is not possible in the space permitted here to trace the paths of the various columns, or to follow the adventures of their commanders, Fergusson, Calvert, and company; these stories deserve their separate volumes. One of Wingate's columns was ambushed and a second scattered before he got astride the railway. Then for several hours the gorges echoed with the thunder of explosion and the crash of rock and metal as one bridge after another was blown up. This demolition fury was crowned when the raiders blasted the side of Bonchaung Gorge, bringing thousands of tons of cliffside down on to the track. Over a length of thirty miles they cut the railway in more than seventy-five places.

Wingate had completed the first phase of his mission with speed and precision. So he then resolved to tackle the second objective, the Mandalay-Lashio railway. It involved the crossing of the Irrawaddy, and for this hazardous operation he dispersed his columns over a wide field. They crossed the river safely, though the Japanese were now buzzing like an angry wasps' nest. The Japanese believed Wingate had a whole division in their rear. They were also apprehensive of the Chinese massing in Yunnan, for they had already themselves mounted a sizeable offensive against the Kachin guerrillas around Sumprabum, eighty miles beyond Myitkyina. These native levies were reinforced by a battalion of the Burma Regiment, led by Lieutenant-Colonel Gamble and based on Fort Hertz, a strong-point which the Allies never gave up in the far north of Burma. Supplied entirely by air-drop, the garrison of Fort Hertz and its patrols carried on unrelenting partisan warfare.

But difficulties began to accumulate for Wingate. Not only did the enemy assemble a force several times outnumbering his own, but the RAF supply dropping, which had so far worked without a hitch, became less certain in the broad open tracts beyond the Irrawaddy, for having made their signals, units had been forced to move before the aircraft could reach them with supplies. The heat was intense, there was a shortage of water, and the sickness rate was rising. Many of the mules had been killed and a number of them eaten, and the tired troops now bore their pack-animals' burdens. Wingate knew that the endurance of his force was running out.

Reluctantly, he abandoned his design against the Mandalay-Lashio railway and broke his force up into dispersal groups with orders to make their several ways back to India. This manoeuvre had been an integral part of their training, and it worked in practice.

Most of the groups reached the Chindwin near Sittaung, where they came under the shield of 23rd Indian Division. Others came out of Burma farther north; one daringly marched eastward, crossed the Salween and reached China. The Chinese people fêted them, and the Americans flew them home to India. By June 1943 the Wingate expedition was over.

It had been a heroic enterprise. All officers and men who took part in it marched not less than 750 miles, and most of them did 1,000 miles. They accomplished this feat in ten to twelve weeks. Their path lay not along roads or even tracks, but through the jungle and over a mass of formless hills. The effort of marching a mile across such country would equal three or four miles on a road. Every man carried on his back about 70lbs of pack, or roughly half his own weight. Oddly enough (though as Wingate had predicted) the prolonged strain prevented the appearance of disease at the time, but it left the body weakened at the end of the campaign. It must be remembered that the men who performed these prodigies were mostly factory hands, clerks, and town-bred labourers. About one-third of them did not return. The Burmese troops who accompanied the expedition proved to be invaluable both as guides and jungle fighters.

Was it a success? Wingate duly claimed that 'a weapon has been found which may well prove a counter to the obstinate but unimaginative courage of the Japanese soldier and which will give scope to the military qualities which the British soldier still shares with his ancestors. These qualities, hitherto unsuspected

'We should land up about here'. Brigadier Orde Wingate created the Chindits. He planned their long-range penetrations behind enemy lines and gave guerilla tactics a new and spectacular twist. He discusses the route to be taken with one of his staff officer Brigade Majors.

by the world, are firstly intelligence in action, that is, originality in individual fighting, and secondly, on the moral side, self-reliance and the power to give of his best when the audience is smallest.'

As for the Japanese, Wingate's raiding operation confirmed the experience of commanders who had met this enemy in pitched battle. Said Wingate, 'His mind is slow but methodical. He is a reasoned, if humourless, student of war in all its phases. He has carefully thought out the answer to all ordinary problems. He hates a leap in the dark to such an extent that he will do anything rather than make it.'

The orthodoxy of the Japanese made it possible for Wingate's commanders to predict with accuracy the enemy's reaction to any move on their part, by no means a universal condition in warfare. When the Japanese were faced with any situation they could not comprehend, their instinct was to withdraw. On the other hand, when they believed they knew the strength and intention of the forces opposing them, the Japanese fought with the utmost courage and determination. They went to the limit to discover these facts. Since they were not usually ascertainable until after a good many hours, the British columns were able to strike camp and vanish into the jungle before the Japanese blow could be directed against them.

General Wingate summed up the achievements of the expedition in these words: 'A considerable force entered Japanese-occupied Burma through a front requiring to be held by an army corps, penetrated to a depth of 200 miles, smashed up a vital line of communication, arrested a Japanese threat to the north already developing, occupied many times its own number of Japanese troops, diverted the enemy's attention and confused his plans. Above all, while doing so they demonstrated a new method of warfare suited to the genius of the United Nations and correspondingly difficult for the Axis to adopt.'

Against this estimate some critics held that the Wingate expedition achieved very little at high cost. Perhaps the soundest way to assess its profit and loss is by the test indicated in the last sentence of Wingate's summing-up. Did his experiment in 1943 make possible his achievement in 1944? The Chindit operations in 1944, with their bearing upon the general campaign, were of unquestionable value, though of moral as much as physical quality. Judged by this standard, Wingate's pioneer venture was justified.

OPERARTION THURSDAY

ON THE EVENING of Sunday, 5 March 1944, a dozen officers on an Indian airfield near Lalaghat pored over a set of aerial reconnaissance photographs. These had been brought in a few minutes earlier by a pilot flying back on a mission which had taken him 200 miles over Japanese territory. On the air-strip, columns of troops in field kit were already lining up to enter a fleet of glider carriers. Some had stowed themselves inside. They were armed with rifles, tommy-guns, pistols, mortars, grenades and knives. These soldiers wore green battledress, and many were bearded.

They were men of the Special Force, otherwise known as the 3rd Indian Division, Long Range Penetration Groups, and still better known as Wingate's Chindits. They were so named by him after the Chinthay, mythical griffin, half-lion, half-eagle guardian of the Burmese temples.

The title '3rd Indian Division' was, in fact, a deception intended for the enemy. Most of its troops were British, drawn from the former 70th Division; the remainder were Gurkhas and West Africans. There were also some American engineer units. The pilots, who were revving up their engines, belonged to No.1 Air Commando, nicknamed on the front as Cochran's Circus. The enterprise in which they were jointly engaged was known in security language as 'Operation *Thursday*. It involved flying 10,000 men and 1,000 pack-animals over the mountain jungle, by night, far beyond the enemy lines, and setting them down in natural clearings in the heart of Burma. If you had raked the earth you would not have found two leaders better qualified to carry through this operation than Wingate and Cochran.

Wingate had much developed his ideas of jungle warfare since his 1943 march into Burma. That had been in the nature of a reconnaissance in force; this was to be an invasion. Then, the troops had gone in on foot and had been supplied by air-drop. Now, the troops themselves were to be flown in. The 1943 expedition had been a series of raids against communications by lightly-armed bands, a game of ambush, booby-traps, and melting away again into the shadows. For his 1944 campaign, Wingate proposed to erect strongholds deep in the enemy zone,

Survivors of the first Wingate expedition 1943.

and, once established, to launch large-scale operations around these fortified bases. It involved flying in not only mobile columns and garrison troops, signal installations, ack-ack and 25-pounder batteries for jungle fortress defence, but also engineer units equipped with bulldozers and mechanical graders to construct airfields capable of handling a regular air supply service. However remote the selected sites might be, the enemy was sure to discover and attack them within a few days. So, the sappers had to work fast.

In his own phrase, Wingate aimed 'to insert himself in the guts of the enemy'. Initially, this was to be accomplished by going not where the enemy was, but where he was not. To neutralise the Japanese airfields in North Burma, for example, it would have been necessary to seize them by airborne landings, and this would certainly be stoutly resisted. Far better to pierce the vulnerable arteries which sustained four enemy divisions in the field and a still respectable air force.

The full policy of Long Range Penetration did not take shape in Wingate's brain overnight. He lived long with it, altering, adapting and rejecting many an idea. At the Quebec Conference, Wingate drummed on continually about the need for developing airborne supply. This had been one-way traffic during his first expedition. Then, to be shot in the leg was often worse luck than being shot through the head, for the foot-slogging columns could not carry their wounded

Chindit radio, 1943.

along with them. But suppose you could evacuate your casualties by air?

Mountbatten realised that this – and much else that they debated – would require special air units. When General Arnold inquired how he might aid the new South-East Asia Command, Mountbatten put forward this suggestion. Arnold at once acceded, and assigned Colonel Philip Cochran and Colonel Robert Alison, two of his star pilots, to work out the details. No.1 Air Commando was born, so named in compliment to the former Chief of Combined Ops. Wingate recorded that 'had this unique force not been provided the operation could never have been carried out'.

In Cochran's Circus, South-East Asia Command found men who had mastered both the art of lifting and towing gliders and the more intricate practice of 'snatching' gliders off the ground by tugs already in the air. The value of this technique in evacuating wounded from inaccessible glades and paddy-fields would be demonstrated hundreds of times in the coming campaign. Cochran was himself a pilot of exceptional skill and daring, who at the age of 33 had become the legendary hero of 'Flip Corkran's Adventures' in American newspaper serials. He proved to be a loyal and imaginative comrade of Wingate.

Long Range Penetration has two requisites: (i) power to penetrate deeply; (ii) power to stay there. Though Wingate set a limit to the period that men could endure the conditions his campaign would impose, he intended to relieve and replace them, not to withdraw the Force itself.

Before these operations could begin, there was a further service Wingate required of the air forces. Would they sweep the sky clear of all interfering enemy aircraft, and keep it so? The co-ordinating air control of Operation *Thursday* had been placed in the hands of Air Marshal Sir John Baldwin, Commander of 3rd Tactical Air Force, and he not only covered the enemy airfields but arranged deception sorties to simulate night landings in areas remote from the real landings.

The bombers of Strategic Air Force (led by Major-General Howard C. Davidson, USAAF) ranged over Rangoon and the Irrawaddy River ports. They dealt such blows that the Japanese seem to have suspected Lower Burma was about to be invaded. Every enemy effort to discover by deep reconnaissance what was really afoot was defeated by the Spitfires of the RAF's Nos. 221 and 224 Groups, and to this sure shield Operation *Thursday* owed much of its success.

Meanwhile, around the chosen landing grounds, Cochran scorched a wide aerial fire-belt, driving back the Japanese fighters from their advanced bases. The pilots of his P.51 Mustangs loaded 1,000lb bombs under each wing, and went in to low-level attack. In these initial strafes and in their unflagging co-operation with the Chindits after the invasion had been launched, Cochran's Circus discharged a million-and-a-half pounds of explosives on the enemy.

Everything was now set for D-Day of the first Allied airborne invasion. Five brigades, amounting almost to the bayonet strength of a couple of divisions, were to be set down on three landing grounds, code-named *Piccadilly*, *Broadway* and *Chowringhee*. These clearings (they were no more) were situated in the triangle Mogaung-Indaw-Bhamo, and had been earmarked by Wingate from the ground-floor during 1943.

The plan was that the first wave of troop-carrying gliders should land, signalling to those following if the enemy was found to be in unexpected possession. Once the gliders had cast off their tow-ropes, of course, they had to go in – and, once in, they had to stay in. The tow-ships, stripped bare to haul the heavy loads, had hardly petrol enough after release to get themselves home over the hostile jungle. The first wave would occupy the clearing, fan out, and screen it while the second wave arrived. This would contain more troops, bulldozers and graders, and also combat engineers to build an air-strip between dawn and dusk, so that the next night the C-47 Dakota aircraft could bring in an army, with its guns, wagons, jeeps, animals and heavy wireless sets.

Once established in this region, the Chindit columns would strike against the railway, road and river systems which served the Japanese army operating against Stilwell's Chinese-American forces. These were approaching from the north through the Hukawng Valley, hauling their Ledo Road with them. To guard Stilwell's right flank, one of Wingate's Brigades (the 16th, commanded by Brigadier Bernard Fergusson DSO) had been marching for a month through the Naga Hills on the west, parallel with his line of advance. They were now nearing the invasion area. Cochran sent off a photo-reconnaissance pilot for a last look round.

And then – disaster. The photographs disclosed that huge trees had been felled across *Piccadilly*, so that no landing there was possible. Had Operation *Thursday* been betrayed at the eleventh hour? *Broadway* was still clear, as the same set of photographs showed, but how long would it remain so? Or, perhaps it would be left clear – and ambushed? For a moment Wingate questioned if the operation could now be mounted at all. But General Slim, who was present with Stratemeyer, Baldwin, Cochran and Old, firmly intervened against postponement. The enemy undoubtedly knew of *Piccadilly*, where the landing of a Dakota had been photographed in the American magazine *Life* the previous year. It was reasonable to assume that the log obstruction of this clearing was no more than a routine precaution. Said Slim, who rarely revealed either elation or depression, 'things are seldom as bad as they seem'. The effect on morale of a postponement had also to be weighed. The risk was calculated, and taken. Cochran walked off to re-brief his crews.

The order was to switch to *Broadway* the troops who had been bound for *Piccadilly*. The landing on *Chowringhee* was scheduled for the following night. It seemed unlikely that the total of eighty gliders could be landed on a single strip during the hours of darkness, but as many as possible were to be launched.

How to explain the change of plan to the crews, who for weeks past had been briefed and rehearsed with maps and models of *Piccadilly*, and now had to be told that their mission must be carried out in a new and strange area? With superb sense of leadership Cochran began, 'I say, boys, we've found a better place to go to'.

An hour after the hitch had occurred, the tugs rolled up the runway to their start lines. The first gliders, towed in pairs, were harnessed. The tugs' engines roared up, and the machines were cast loose. Bouncing, swaying, and straining, the aerial train rushed down the strip in a whirlwind of dust, hauled itself up over the trees, and set forth over the 8,000-foot mountain barrier for the heart of enemy-held Burma. It was twelve minutes past six o'clock.

So began a movement which was, until the invasion of Fortress Europe in June 1944, the greatest airborne adventure of the war. Long after night had come the tugs continued taking off from Lalaghat at five-minute intervals. They were within radio call of their base, and linked by telephone with their gliders. Not one in twenty of the airborne troops had ever flown before. No fighters escorted the air armada, which travelled without lights and had been ordered to land by no other illumination than that of the moon. All depended on surprise – and no man knew what lay at the end of his journey.

Over *Broadway*, the tugs circled to pick out the dark strip between the trees. Then – 'Good luck! and the gliders cast off and went in.

Of the sixty-seven gliders that flew, thirty-two landed on *Broadway*. None were hit by anti-aircaft fire, though several were fired on; nine came down in the enemy lines, eleven on friendly soil. The other fifteen were turned back by signal because of the congestion on *Broadway* and returned safely to their base.

The crashes and crash-landings between the two points were due to the parting of tow-ropes unable to bear the strain of the double loads. Some of these accidental descents had an unexpected value, for they occurred almost on top of a Japanese divisional headquarters, 100 miles from the scene of operations. The enemy could not have been unaware of the exceptional traffic overhead that night, for the sky was filled with the roar of engines. But when his sentries were fired on, he seems to have been misled into believing that a series of flying Commando raids was taking place.

Meanwhile, all had not gone according to plan at *Broadway*. The advance party gliders had landed, but the Control Glider had been forced down on the banks of the

Chindwin River. No guiding brain, therefore, directed the procession of arrival on the strip. Lacking a ground control, gliders overshot the mark and ploughed through the deceptive ground beyond, which was cut up by timber-hauling ruts and buffalo-holes overgrown with grass. Other gliders came to grief on the strip itself, and, as they piled up, the next arrivals crashed into them. On the crowded runway, men heaved frantically and tore their muscles dragging the wrecks clear. Then the cry would rise again, terrible in its urgency, 'Gliders!' The next wave was diving in.

One glider, loaded with a bulldozer and other heavy machinery, whipped over sharply to avoid a wreck and plunged into the wall of the jungle at 60 mph. On either side the trees tore off its wings, the fuselage rushed on with its load, by now wrenched loose from its moorings. When the fuselage halted at last, the bulldozer continued its momentum. This worked the hinge by which the pilots' seat is swung upward to let the vehicle drive out. Pilot and co-pilot were thrown into the air, the bulldozer shot out beneath them, and they landed back unhurt. 'I planned it just that way,' the American pilot is reported to have claimed.

But there were grim scenes, too, where the surgeons amputated by light of the moon, and there were gliders that crashed far beyond in the jungle with a frightful cry – and then silence fell while men hunted frantically in the darkness for their dying comrades.

The casualties were lighter than anyone dared expect. Twenty-three men were dead, and as many injured. Four hundred troops and many stores had been delivered. But almost all the mechanical equipment, so necessary for clearing away the debris quickly, had been lost. Brigadier Calvert, whose 77th Brigade was the spearhead of the air invasion, decided to halt all further traffic towards him. At first light the engineers of the US Army's 900th Field Unit began to level the surface by hand.

Thirteen hours later the first Troop Carrier Command transport landed safely, bringing reinforcements and evacuating the injured. That night fifty-five Dakotas came in to *Broadway*. This transportation continued without hitch or interference by the enemy for five more nights.

Meanwhile, the gliders had opened up a second branch at *Chowringhee*, south of the Irrawaddy bend (*Broadway* and *Piccadilly* both lay north of the bend), and with the same speed four columns of Brigadier W.D.A. Lentaigne's 111th Brigade, with its headquarters, were carried in.

The operations of Troop Carrier Command were supervised (and its hazardous first flights led) by General Old, who long ago had made himself familiar with these landing grounds by flying low over them in moonlight. His transport service worked so smoothly that one illegitimate passenger, bound for Imphal, found it more convenient to fly from Lalaghat via *Broadway* than by the recognised route. The Dakotas made 660 sorties and the gliders seventy-eight; they transported 9,052 troops, 1,360 pack-animals and 250 tons of equipment, at a casualty cost of 121 men. Not a single Dakota was lost. Four days after they had landed, the columns were marching off along the jungle paths to start their respective assaults on the Japanese communications.

Wingate was determined not to sit upon the doorstep of his achievement. The approach of Fergusson's marching brigade had raised his strength to 12,000 combat troops. They were planted, in truth, 'in the guts of the enemy', and not yet been located by him. But this period of immunity was rapidly running out. Wingate gave the order to abandon *Chowringhee* and move across the Irrawaddy towards a new stronghold which he had planned about forty miles west of the railway. It was named *Aberdeen*, after his wife's home.

It was not too soon. The Japanese at last reacted. Two hours after the rearguard of Lentaigne's brigade had withdrawn from *Chowringhee*, the enemy bombed and strafed the burnt-out gliders on that abandoned strip. Within a few days Fergusson had hacked a clearing at *Aberdeen*, and on 23 March a fourth Chindit brigade (the 14th, commanded by Brigadier Tom Brodie) was flying in. Operation *Thursday* was over.

It was Wingate's last, as it was his finest, exploit. Tragedy set a seal upon his triumph. Flying towards India the next evening, his aircraft was lost in a storm. An American pilot, landing about midnight, reported that he had seen a machine crash in flames on a mountainside in the Naga lands. Air and ground reconnaissance parties went out, and eventually found the charred remains of a Mitchell bomber. Thirty yards away from the wreckage lay Wingate's battered 'coal-scuttle' topee, which had been a landmark to every man in his command. With this singular soldier perished the American crew and two British war correspondents, Stuart Emeny of *The News Chronicle* and Stanley Wills of *The Daily Herald*.

What Wingate might ultimately have accomplished will never be known. Mystery, and mysticism, too, threaded the man's life. You could never quite distinguish where the real and the romantic merged in him. He acted, and also exhibited, as when he walked around with an alarm-clock dangling from a chain and ringing periodically 'to remind people that time was passing'. He survived his adventures long enough to impose much of his pattern on the jungle war. Some critics complained that his Special Force or 'Private Army' was an extravagant venture; there is no doubt he demanded (and obtained) for it unusually generous supply. Others considered that there should be no 'specialising' anyway, but that all troops in the Burma theatre should be equally well trained and equipped. This was a sincere if unintended tribute to 'the Man', as Cochran called him.

His Command devolved on Brigadier Lentaigne DSO, one of his most trusted lieutenants.

THE WAR OF THE CHINDITS

IT WOULD BE too complicated to chart the movements of Lentaigne's thirty-odd columns, for some of them marched a dozen times over the same track. The story of Fergusson's brigade may be taken as representative of the experiences of the Chindits.

It was 5 February 1944, when Fergusson, a blue-eyed, six-foot Highlander, monocle firmly screwed in his eye, led his men out of Ledo in the valley of the Upper

Brahmaputra under the shoulder of the Hump. They included men of the Queen's, Leicesters, Reconnaissance Regiment, Royal Artillery and Royal Signals. The Recce men had discarded their motors and the artillerymen their guns; marching across these unmapped mountains with gradients of one-in-one they proved themselves equal to the sturdiest infantry. The youngest of Fergusson's men was 19 years of age; the oldest was 45.

No trails led to the south; the Chindits made their own. Often they had to carve a path through the undergrowth with machetes, relieving the relays of sweating men at the head of the column every three or four minutes. Some days they advanced only a couple of miles.

The hills were so steep that men had to crawl on hands and knees, and they were so slippery with the rain that pours in torrents in this region, the wettest on earth, that even the mules fell. Fergusson reported: 'It was the worst track I ever saw animals go over. I do not recall any stretch of level going more than a hundred yards in length.' With the brigade, all the way from Ledo, marched their mascot bull, Oscar the Chindit. He carried sick and wounded men on his back, and was beloved.

Orde Wingate without beard.

Fergusson's men were equipped with the same kind of kit as Wingate's pioneer expedition, and relied even more on air supply. Few human beings inhabit this desolate tract, and for many days they did not even sight a Japanese person. Level areas, suitable for supply-drop, were not easily found, and rations and ammunition would come parachuting down only to get caught in the topmost branches of the trees. Then a marksman would be called for to shoot the bundle free – a delicate operation when a case of grenades was involved.

At other times hungry troops would hear the roar of 'planes circling overhead in the mist, and even see them diving with fearful risk through the grey shroud to find the men they were supplying. Then down would float the precious load – only to have the wind lift it at the last moment as it was about to land, and drop it gently over the edge of the precipice. Men then had to pull in their belts and make three days' rations last for five. Food means much to soldiers at all times. Tramping through an evil-smelling jungle, drenched by rain, dried-out by noonday's sun, drenched again by night's heavy dew, food (and tobacco) became an obsession.

When the Chindits crossed a jungle track each man made his own way so as not to wear a path. The rear platoon swept dust over the footprints. The men worked in pairs in almost every form of activity, fighting, marching, making a bivouac, cooking, eating and washing.

They had covered 100 miles in this fashion before they came to the tawny Chindwin, the river they must cross to enter into the heart of the Japanese domain.

An eye-witness describes how the first marching column emerged from the jungle in single file, hungry, weary, weighted down with equipment, leading their mules and oxen. They trudged to the water's edge, and as dusk fell camp fires sprang up along the fringe of the trees. The drone of aircraft sounded.

At the first throb of the engines all flames were doused. The 'plane wheeled overhead flashing a message, to which the bivouac made answer with a lamp. Then suddenly petrol fires blazed up in the form of a huge letter L, the first aircraft roared down over their heads, and out of its dark hull came a cascade of sacks. They contained letters from home, food, ammunition, cigarettes, newspapers, even snuff and spectacles.

It was the job of the Leicesters to build the bridgehead on the far side of the Chindwin, but where were the bridges – or boats? Again the planes came, towing gliders high above the river, bringing rubber boats with outboard motors. They landed on a sandbank and unloaded, and a few minutes later the Leicesters had set up their bridgehead without a single casualty. 'Hannibal eclipsed!' cried Wingate, who came in with Cochran in a light aircraft to inspect them. The march continued, making a detour to destroy the Japanese garrison at the jade-mine centre of Lonkin. By mid-March, as we have seen, the brigade had arrived at *Aberdeen* and fortified it.

Turning south-east then, Fergusson launched a surprise attack on Indaw, a built-up area of dumps, vehicle parks and aircraft on the Mandalay-Myitkyina railway. It was this railway which supplied the enemy forces in North Burma opposing Stilwell's advance from Ledo down the Mogaung Valley.

The assault was made by men who had covered eighty miles in the previous five days. For half of this time they had been without fresh water, and wounded men had drunk rusty container water used to cool the machine-guns. Indeed, the fighting at Indaw circled round the desperate effort of the Chindits to force their way down to the banks of the Meza River. It was in vain. From well-sited bunkers the enemy covered every approach with machine-guns, and our men suffered the agony of seeing, almost touching, the water and being denied the taste of one drop of it.

It had been one of the British objectives to occupy the air-strip at Indaw. But the Japanese were able to concentrate rapidly along the railway from either end, and though Brodie joined with Fergusson they did not together possess the strength to seize and hold Indaw. It was not the primary role of Long Range Penetration troops to fight prolonged engagements away from their strongholds. They did battle with the equipment they carried on their backs. And so, with ammunition and rations running low, the two brigades drew off from Indaw. In all, Fergusson's men marched 600 miles. Though his operation achieved no great strategic success, as an example of courage and endurance this march will rank with the finest of all time.

In the meantime, Calvert's brigade had marched out of *Broadway*, and, striking westward, also assailed the railway. At Henu his men erected their famous road-rail block of 'White City', which had been better named 'Red City', from the blood that flowed there. It was imperative for the Japanese to remove this block, which was throttling the life out of their troops in the Mogaung Valley. They brought up light tanks and 150mm 'coal-scuttle' mortars to support their infantry. Calvert's gunners replied with 25-pounders and Bofors. A ferocious battle followed.

Men of the South Staffs, Lancashire Fusiliers and 6th Gurkhas attacked with bayonet and rifle-butt. The Gurkhas and West Africans engaged with their native knives, the Japanese with their traditional two-handed swords. An incessant rain of grenades burst over the heads of the fighters and among the groups inextricably mixed up in personal combat. 'Mad Mike' Calvert, with fixed bayonet, led the Gurkhas forward. An officer who was there describes White City battle as 'mediaeval'. Its characteristic was its savagery.

'The conduct of our troops,' said this officer, 'was beyond all praise. The Staffords had to advance up a gradient of one-in-two in the teeth of murderous machine-gun and rifle fire. They went up that hill as steadily as if they had been on manoeuvre. Many scores of bodies lie there, with faces shot away, testifying what they went through. But they reached the crest and took no prisoners. Japanese snipers still swing in the trees to which they had lashed themselves before they died.' The battle continued through the night, while overhead the air transports went on delivering supplies.

One of the RAF Sections that went into Japanese-occupied Burma with the Chindits. (Historic Military Press)

At dawn it was seen that the Japanese were digging themselves in on a hill overlooking White City. Immediately an assault was launched to dislodge them. The cost was high. When the general counter-attack was unleashed, the enemy fled, leaving his wounded on the ground. But he came back, time and again, striving furiously to break the grip on his communications.

An eyewitness described how the Japanese rushed blindly into minefields and over booby-traps and were blown to pieces or else mown down like autumn corn by riflemen and machine-gunners. Howling like hyenas, they piled up on to the wire, which by morning was festooned with bodies, many of them stripped naked by the explosions from mortars and grenades. Scores were killed by their own Bangalore torpedoes, which they carried to blow gaps in the barricades.

At a crisis of the battle, Cochran's Air Commandos planted a load of high-explosives on Japanese concentrations preparing to move up. The pilots had been reluctant; so short was the distance separating the forces that they feared to hit their own men. But urged by the troops and guided to their targets by RAF pilots serving with them on the ground as 'spotters' (also known as Forward Observation Officers) at visual control-posts, they unloaded on the enemy everything they had, destroying hundreds. Visual control-posts later became a widely used device for calling up aircraft to bomb or strafe enemy positions which were checking the attack. White City was never taken by the Japanese, though in May the Chindits abandoned it on establishing a new jungle Tobruk further up the railway line in the Hopin Valley. This was at *Blackpool*, thirty miles south-west of Mogaung.

Blackpool was the stamping ground of Lentaigne's old 111th Brigade, the 'Ghost Force'. They included the soldiers from the Cameronians, King's Own Royal Regiment, as well as troops of two Gurkha units and the Royal Artillery. After their withdrawal from *Chowringhee* they had crossed the Irrawaddy and moved towards Bhamo at the same time that a mixed British and Kachin force struck down along the Chinese frontier to cut the Bhamo-Myitkyina road. This latter force actually entered China at one point, reappearing to operate against Myitkyina from the east. Lentaigne's brigade returned to harass the enemy, who were desperately holding on to Mogaung and Kamaing. Following an eighty-mile march over the mountains they descended on Hopin. There they were within a few minutes' aircraft flight of the Japanese front line against Stilwell.

The Japanese struck back violently against this new challenge. For two weeks they flung strong forces against the post. In the final assault, which began on 23 May, they brought up 105mm and 75mm artillery. During one bombardment 300 shells fell inside the perimeter within an hour. The garrison gave up its airstrip and prepared to fight it out. It meant sacrificing the service most valued by the troops (and most uplifting to them) – the flying-out of their wounded. The hard decision had to be made. As it was, with superior strength, both in men and arms, the Japanese broke through the perimeter and contested the possession of the commanding hills. But now the time of the monsoon had come and as the clouds closed in, precluding further airborne supplies, the brigade evacuated *Blackpool*.

They had fought for twenty days and nights, and now faced a march through the morass of the Indaw Valley towards the hills around Mogaung. They tied their wounded on their backs and set forth, slashing a path through the elephant-grass, hacking footholds up and down precipices of mud, wading along tracks which had become torrents.

By this time the whole front was ablaze, for the Japanese had delivered their last and greatest attack on India a few days after Operation *Thursday* had been launched. The airborne invasion of Burma, which had captured the imagination of the world by its novelty and daring, receded in interest as it merged in the general campaign of the Fourteenth Army. The battles at Kohima and Imphal, where the main power of the Japanese Army was held, and broken, took centre stage, and the marching and manoeuvring of the Chindits in the mysterious forests beyond the Chindwin were obscured.

Their contribution to the defeat of the Japanese on the Ledo front was considerable. For three out of five months they blocked the railway to Myitkyina, the main Japanese base in North Burma. Rarely did the enemy risk sending up a large convoy. A few motor transports would make a dash for it at night, running the gauntlet to their own front line. The Chindits spotted one troop train moving along in daylight; they called up the air force, which came over the hills from Imphal and wiped it out.

As important as any military operations, the Chindits demonstrated once more that British and Indian troops can fight back long after the enemy consider that they have had enough. 'I do not believe the British soldier is braver than any other,' says Slim, 'but he is brave for longer, and it is the extra ten minutes that count'.

The Chindit badge worn by Corporal 6093146 George Edward Archer during his service in the 2nd Queen's Royal Regiment (West Surrey). The regiment participated in the second Chindit expedition (Operation *Thursday*), as part of 16th Brigade. The brigade was formed into eight columns, two of which consisted of 2nd Queen's, No.21 column commanded by Lieutenant Colonel Metcalfe and No.22 commanded by the Second-in-Command, Major T.V. Close. Each column consisted of 400 men, seventy-five mules and twelve ponies, the latter mainly for carrying casualties. The columns were to be re-supplied by airdrop every five days. The name of the Chindits originated from a suggestion by Captain Aung Thin DSO of the Burma Rifles and was based on the Burmese mythical beast Chinthé or Chinthya, statues of which guard Buddhist temples. (Historic Military Press)

The soldiers of these roving columns needed that quality of endurance above all. They had to carry their household on their back – food, blankets, cooking utensils, medical gear, besides their weapons and ammunition. They possessed pack-animals, but there were heavy wireless sets, mortars, and wounded men to be strapped on these or placed on a ring-saddle, and there is a limit to the number of mules that a column can usefully employ.

Sickness and wounds were the hardest problem. Malaria was impossible to avoid. You cannot wear a mosquito-net while marching, and if you wear a veil it is torn to pieces. On the other hand, if you smear yourself with anti-mosquito cream it stops up your pores, and you nearly burst from heat exhaustion. Other jungle curses were jaundice, dysentery, scrub-typhus and Naga sores, which turn septic and spread like prairie fire. Some soldiers' backs were blanketed with elastoplast strips to cover these raw patches. Such items are inseparable from jungle war, and troops in all zones suffered from them. But the marching columns far away in the enemy country had to wait for the planes to evacuate their casualties. They owed a double debt to the doctors and medical orderlies who marched with them.

Evacuation by air was the supreme service which Mountbatten's forethought had secured for his Command. Several thousand of the Chindits were brought out to the hospitals and leave centres in India by this method. The pilots flew across mountains three times as high as Snowdon, in storm, darkness and enemy fire. There is weather in these parts which will toss a transport plane upside down, spin it as a leaf in a gale, or tear its wings off. The controls ice, instruments go haywire, water pours in through the joints as by a forced-feed spray, and lightning flashes along the wings and round the airscrew. Such are the conditions that had to be fought to carry out Mountbatten's order 'Fly through the monsoon'.

The pilots would start off from India in cloud down to the level of the tree-tops, cross the frontier mountains without catching a glimpse of them, and emerge over Burma in sunshine – perhaps to find a Japanese fighter waiting for them. Then the message would come through to base 'Zero on my tail, warn all aircraft', and another brave man had gone down.

There was no air recovery service in the jungle at that time. Forced landings were not often possible. You had to bale out, and then you had a 100-mile walk ahead of you. Out of thirty pilots in succession who were forced down, ten successfully made that journey home.

The strangest flying of all was done by a couple of Sunderland flying-boats. The Sunderlands had been designed for submarine patrol work, not to fly over Himalayan mountains. Nor had their pilots been trained for such work. But they stripped off their guns to give their aircraft greater lift and, skimming the trees to creep under the Japanese fighter net, they put down their hulls on Indawgyi Lake in the heart of the jungle. *Gert* and *Daisy* took safely to India more than 600 sick and wounded. When the water was too rough for them to come in, a fleet of outboard motor-boats were used to ply northward up the river to the American lines in the Mogaung Valley. This 'Chindit Navy' evacuated another 1,000 patients.

When the men came out of the jungle after five months they were pretty tired, and they showed it. Bearded troops seem always to look gaunter, and most of these had shed many pounds of weight. They asked first of all for their mail – that blessed letter from home – and may home never forget it.

Wingate had signalled them a day before his death: 'One day you will be proud to say "I was there".' Those who were there and returned will remember others who did not come back. There was the machine-gunner who refused to leave his gun for forty-eight hours, though enemy fire had set the jungle round him blazing and the rubber pipe of his gun was melting. There was the wounded sergeant who twice threw himself from the mule on which his comrades had placed him because he would not slow the march and imperil their chance of getting through a Japanese encirclement. And there was the major who got his fatal bullet at an ambushed well while searching for water for his men. He ordered them to leave him, asked for extra ammunition for his rifle, sent a message to his wife, and remained lying there waiting for his last enemy.

Soldiers and airmen drawn haphazard from the towns and villages of Britain, India, Africa and America, of all kinds and races, and of varying ages, stuck it out through one of the hardest campaigns in history.

WAVELL INSPECTS THE TROOPS

Field Marshal Sir Archibald Wavell, C-in-C India, was a great supporter of the then Brigadier Wingate. Here he is seen with officers of the Chindits. Brigadier Wingate is at extreme right of top photo on the eve of the first expedition into Burma.

Above, right and opposite: Field Marshal Wavell inspecting the men of the Chindits in February 1943 before the start of the first march into Burma.

L to R Lt Gen Brehon B Somervell (Commanding General, US Services of Supply); FM Sir Archibald Wavell; General Raymond A Wheeler (Deputy Supreme Allied Commander under Mountbatten) on a tour of inspection of the Chindit force.

Brig Wingate, FM Wavell, and Gen Somervell.

Above, left and overleaf above: Field Marshal Wavell inspecting the men of the Chindits before the first expedition.

F/M Wavell (then C-in-C India) with Major Mike Calvert RE and Captain JG Lockett. Both men commanded Chindit columns and both would later be awarded the DSO.

F/M Wavell with other staff officers at Imphal 1943.

A reconnaissance boat being used as a ferry to ship stores across the River Chindwin.

F/M Wavell (then C-in-C India) at Imphal, March 1943, prior to the departure of the first Wingate expedition.

Left and below: A jungle printing press operated by Chindit force Burmese patriots preparing a manifesto for the jungle villages.

'We should land up about here'. Brigadier Orde Wingate created the Chindits. He planned their long-range penetrations behind enemy lines and gave guerilla tactics a new and spectacular twist. In these images he can be seen discussing the route to be taken with one of his staff officer Brigade Majors.

Brigadier Wingate, before the start of the campaign, looking thoughtfully at the jungle-covered hills that he and his men would soon climb.

ON THE MARCH

A halt on the march. This is the first of the many Burmese temples passed by the Chindits on their journey.

An example of a full jungle head dress worn by the Chindits in the fly and mosquito-infested jungle through which they passed.

A road block being made to prevent surprise attack during a brief halt.

One of the elephants which formed so valuable a part of the Chindit transport .

Nothing was left to chance. Here a road block is being made to prevent surprise attack during a brief halt.

The 38 year old commander Brigadier Orde Wingate testing his newly sharpened kukri.

Wireless was the men's only communication link between columns and base. This image shows the Signal section of the RAF reporting progress across the Chindwin.

Bullocks were 'borrowed' to help with transport. Here are a few crossing the Chindwin River.

Rubber boats begin to yield a dividend after all the trouble the troops had in carrying them.

Elephants and their mahouts helped to carry equipment and weapons across the Chindwin River.

Crossing the Chindwin River. The troops are approaching Japanese-occupied territory.

EVACUATION!

Men of the Burma Rifles climb into their aircraft for the trip back to India. These men had been cut off on the far side of the Irrawady River and had walked nearly 1,400 miles before entering the friendly Kachin Hill area along the Yunnan-Burma border. They were fortunate enough to contact the Kachin levies and were eventually flown back to India.

Hill tribesmen, interested in the take-off of the rescue aircraft.

Friendly hill tribesmen gathered about the aircraft that will carry off the trekkers.

A broken-down jeep being loaded onto the aircraft.

Emplaning for the homeward journey to India.

At the end of their long jungle trek, exhausted, half-starved and dishevelled, these men still raise a smile.

SUPPLIES FROM THE SKIES

Supplies to the Wingate Expedition were parachuted down by the RAF. Here Indian troops are folding the 18 foot, Indian made, cotton parachutes into the packs which are clipped onto the supply loads.

Rations for Chindits. Left to right: digestive biscuits, dates, cheese, sugar, salt, tea, matches, chocolate, powdered milk, cigarettes. Each tin holds ten days rations. In this picture is a two-day ration.

Somewhere over Burma just before a supply drop.

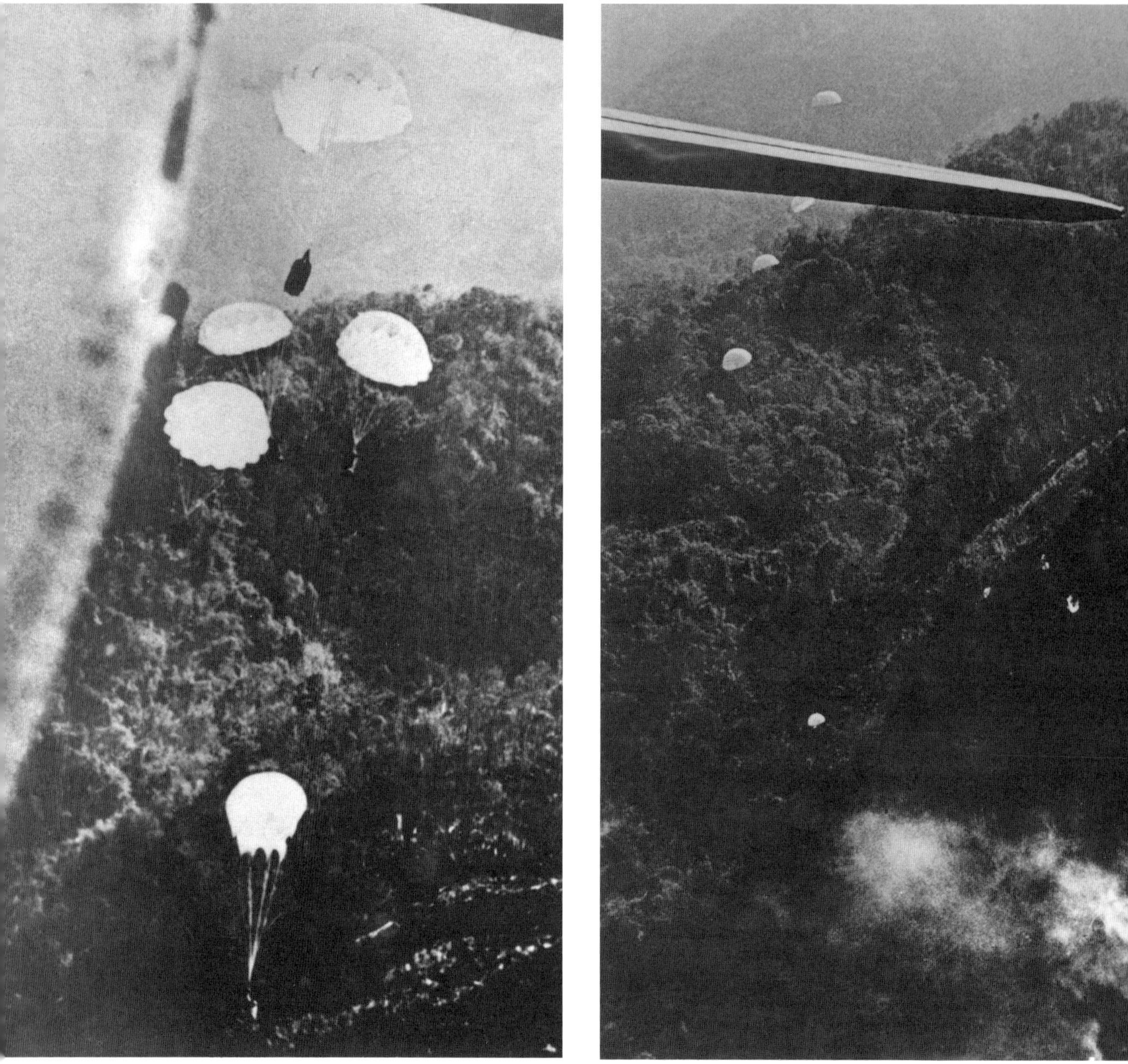

Above left and right: Supplies parachute down to men making their way through some of the most difficult country in the world. The smoke signal is the pilot's guide.

Wingate's men run to pick up parachute loads and collect the chutes with which to form a signal. They are visible only against the sun, otherwise they blend perfectly into the landscape as seen from the air. The men in this picture had been without food for two days.

LIVE TO FIGHT ANOTHER DAY

Of the many stories told of the Wingate Expeditions none was more spectacular than the rescue flight of an RAF transport aircraft which landed on a tiny improvised field deep in the enemy territory on 28 April 1943 to bring out seventeen sick and wounded men who otherwise would never have lived to come back. Writing a message with parachutes: the men signal from their jungle landing ground - "Please land here now". As they came into land the men in the aircraft knew they were running many risks and that they might easily crash when trying to take off again.

Regimental Sergeant Major J Livingstone of the King's Regiment (later awarded the Military Cross) had a most appropriate name as a member of this jungle expedition. Here he is by the tailplane with Company Sergeant Major Richard Cheevers (later awarded the Distinguished Conduct Medal) who was never seen without his Tommy gun.

After the agonising uncertainty of the take-off - they cleared the trees by inches - the rescued men settle down inside the aircraft, the flight rigger passing round a German water can, a souvenir from the Western Desert. The man taking it is suffering from dysentery and an infected hip. He steadies himself by holding on to the static line to which the parachute hooks are fastened.

Lancashire men and a Gurkha private. The Lancashire men were Lance Corporal James Rogerson of Blackburn and Private Jack Wilson of Preston.

The Japanese didn't print this for them. Private William Growhurst from London and Sergeant Tony Aubrey showing a piece of Japanese paper money they picked up in a Burma village.

Back safely on Indian soil, they had covered in a matter of hours a distance that would take their comrades weeks. Here is Corporal Jimmy Walker being helped from the plane.

No longer in a place where he has to keep an eye constantly open for the Japanese, Sergeant Jack Barry re-reading a letter that the RAF had dropped to him in the jungle. "Mail" it was reported he said under his breath "that's what's kept us going, word from home."

Pages 55-57: Supplies parachuted down to men making their way through some of the most difficult country in the world. The smoke signal is the pilot's guide.

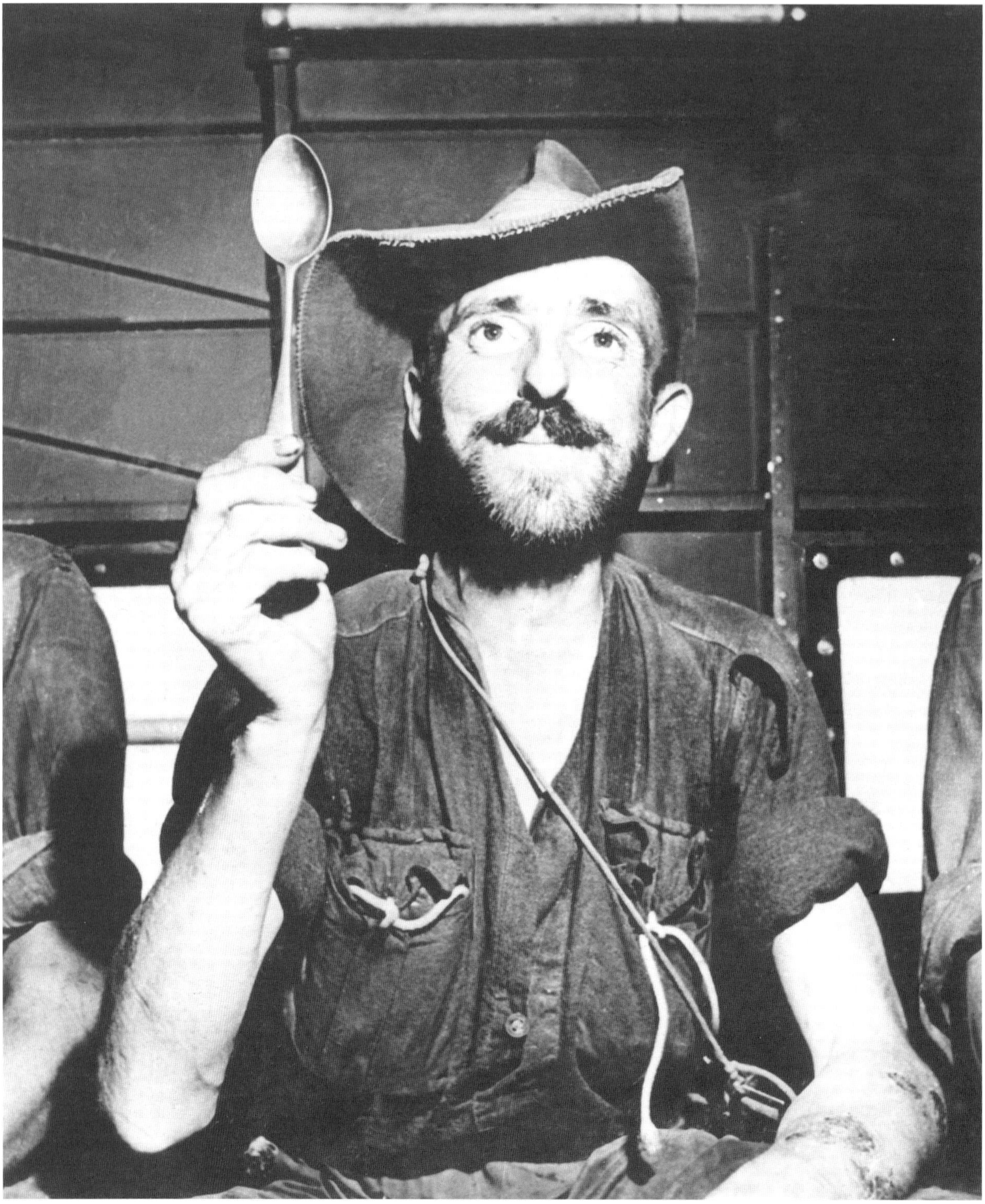

The only spoon, valued more highly than gold.

Pages 59-61: Sick men being evacuated by Dakota from Kohaukewe valley.

SUPPLY LINE FOR 10,000 MEN

Above and opposite: Supplies being packed to be dropped by air.

The packing shed at an air base where supplies are packed ready for air dropping.

Pages 65-68: Supplies being packed in bamboo containers for 'free' dropping by air.

Above and overleaf: Parachutes being packed for dropping supplies by air.

Pages 71-73: These images tell the story of just one supply drop. Here supplies are being loaded into Dakotas for dropping by air.

Pages 74-82: Heavily-laden and well defended against ground anti-aircraft fire, here the Dakotas are in flight and taking supplies to be dropped by air. These trips were vital in keeping the men supplied with food and ammunition.

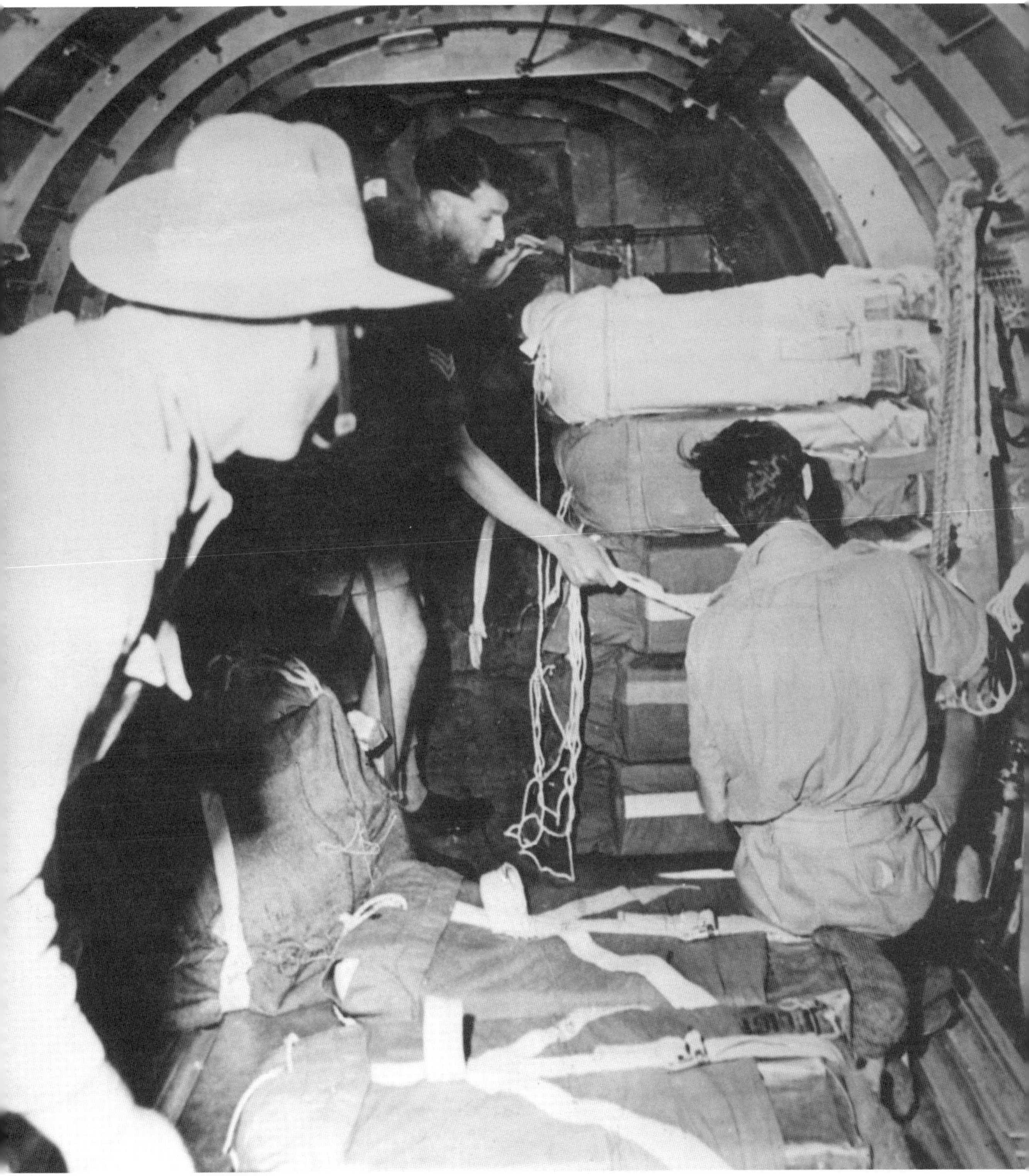

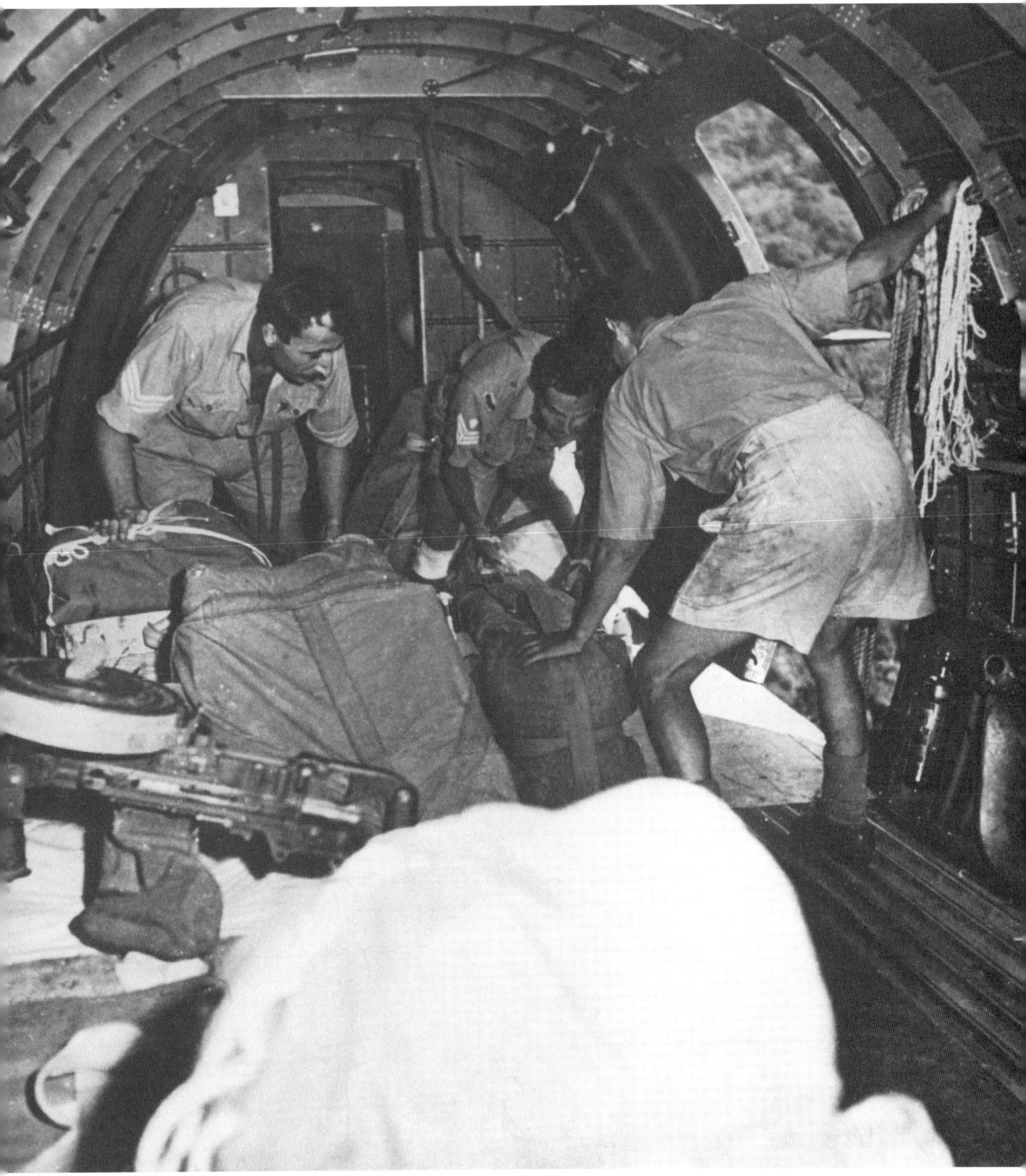

MEN OF THE CHINDITS

It was described in some quarters as a "patrol in strength" but over a period of three months they blew up railway lines, sabotaged Japanese military stores, destroyed bridges and dislocated road transport. Here is a happy group of Chindits after the successful operation.

The beard soon came off, Major Bernard Fergusson.

Above, left and overleaf: Survivors of the first Wingate expedition 1943.

Brigadier Wingate with his men after the expedition.

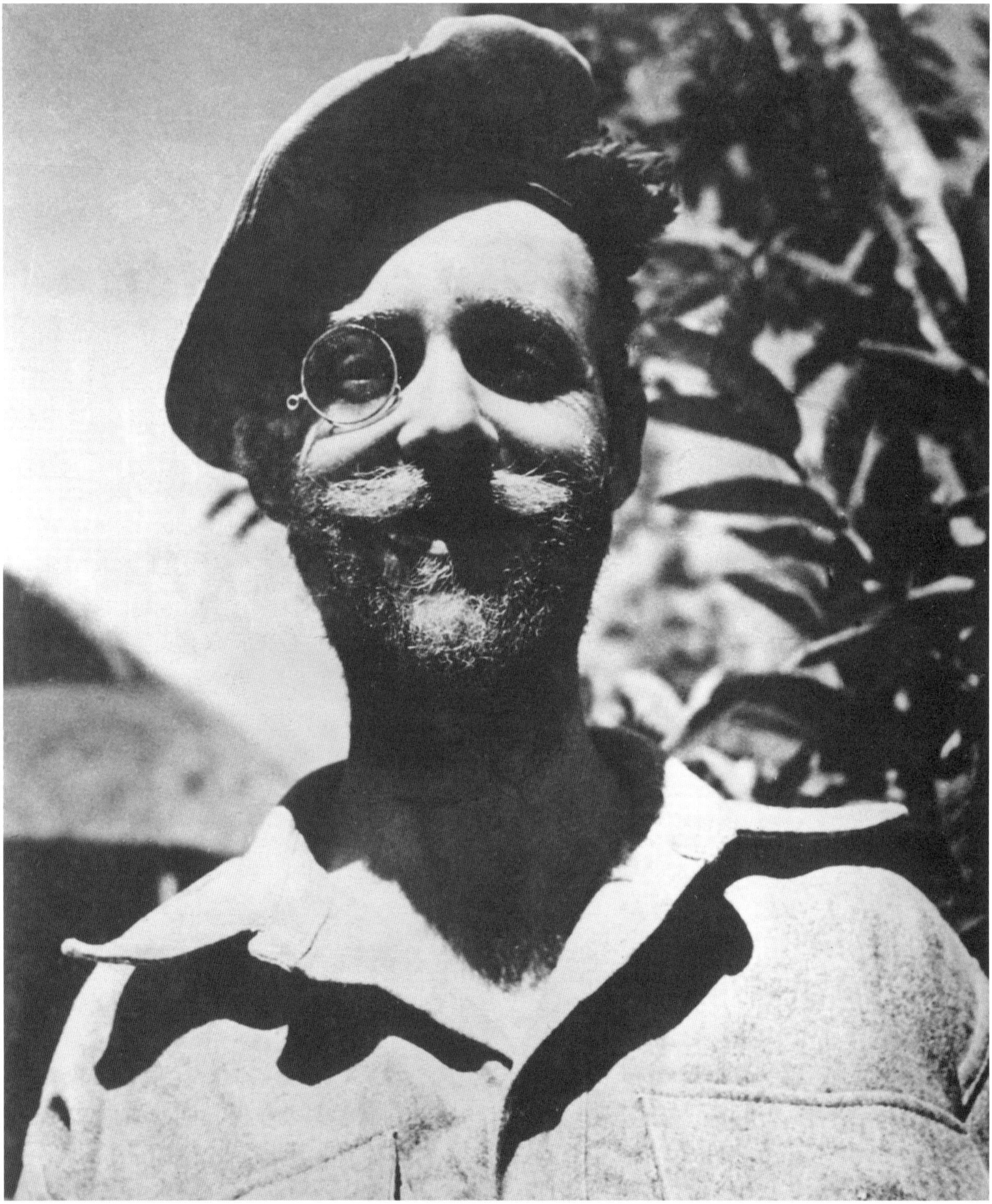

Major Bernard Fergusson, (later awarded the DSO) commanded column 5 and is seen here after his return.

Brigadier Wingate reaching road-head, where a jeep was waiting to return him to the headquarters from where he had started three months earlier.

Brigadier Wingate on his way to the barber.

Brigadier Wingate shaved and changed.

Brigadier Wingate with one of his officers.

Brigadier Wingate being met by one of the divisional commanders on his return.

Officers discussing their experiences with Brigadier Wingate.

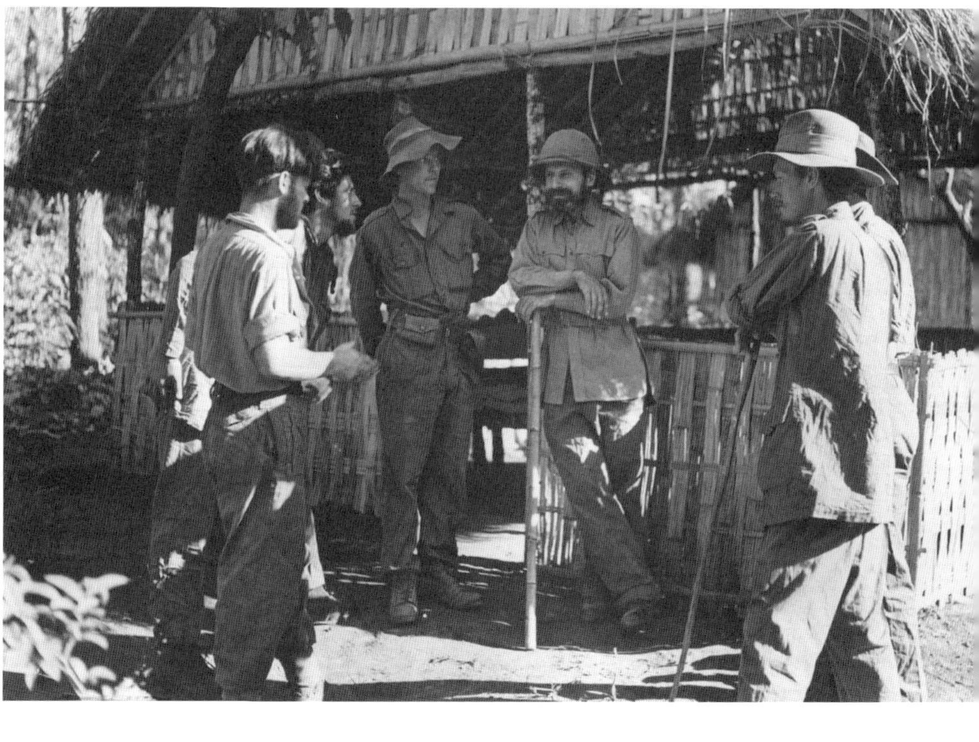

Brigadier Wingate enjoying a joke with one of his officers.

While still on Burmese soil these officers had left their concerns behind in the jungle.

Tired but happy: two British soldiers with a Gurkha comrade. All participated in the campaign.

A Gurkha soldier disguised as a Burman.

These two British soldiers with their Gurkha comrade have bathed and changed. A spot of leave is in their minds.

An official war artist finds a study in an officer who has not yet removed his beard grown during the months of the campaign.

The British ground gunners and General Wingate's forces defending a landing strip deep inside Burma prospect for a gun position near one of Col. Philip Cochrane's burnt-out gliders, which came to grief on the first night of the landing in the jungle clearing.

One of General Wingate's jungle commanders deep in the heart of enemy-occupied Burma.

A patrol of General Wingate's men crossing a stream many miles behind the Japanese lines in the picturesque surroundings of Northern Burma. It may look like a peaceful scene but there were Japanese within a few miles of this place when the picture was taken.

Below left and right: Reviewing information after a routine reconnaissance patrol.

An official war correspondent who followed the expedition.

The second expedition was a much bigger operation. As more territory came under allied control then larger forces were required. Here Gurkha reinforcements are pouring in beyond enemy lines inside Burma. Carrier aircraft continue performing their hazardous tasks unhampered.

The all-American crew of a carrier aircraft after landing on a strip inside Burma.

This American transport aircraft pilot is pointing out a Japanese barracks he intends to bomb in the course of his transport flight. Even while they carried men and material these transport crews did not spare any enemy objectives that came their way.

Spare steel helmets would do just as well. Here, American engineers have their coffee on their arrival inside Burma. They were always amongst first arrivals on a site chosen as a future landing strip and they usually had a strip ready within a few hours of their arrival.

These guns warded off the enemy from one of the allied landing strips.

A bulldozer clearing the airfield by shovelling off masses of earth. The strip must be kept in good repair.

A tractor pulling a leveller supplements this bulldozers's efforts in perfecting the landing strip.

Major TW Robinson of the Royal Engineers detachment on the second expedition photographed in the jungle.

In this photograph, whilst waiting for his lunch Lt. Col. CB Gaty reads the Time of 13 March 1944 which says that the British are evidently going to let another campaigning season pass by without attacking Burma. He was amazed as he sat and read this 200 miles inside Burma.

With his sixty days growth of beard, Flt. Lt. A Stickney Harris of Newcastle, New Brunswick, Canada hardly looked the wireless operator air gunner that he was, with a Catalina squadron operating in Central Burma. He was Air Liaison officer with one of the columns on the march, handling with his wireless set all the business connected with the air supplying carried out from India.

Flt. Lt RH Riddell, aged 21 of Gleichen, Alberta, Canada. The pilot was another of the liaison officers with one of the columns of troops operating inside Burma. He selected suitable spots for airfields and maintained radio communication with his base.

One of the American light aircraft which did such a splendid job of plucking wounded men out from beneath the very noses of the Japanese, is here seen landing at its base in Burma.

Victories could not be gained without casualties. These wounded men were waiting to be evacuated by American aircraft from a base in Burma. In the foreground is Private D Morris from Leeds. He received several machine-gun wounds in the legs and a rifle bullet in the arm on his 31st birthday.

Wounded soldiers in Burma awaiting evacuation to base hospitals in India.

Yet another huge transport carrier landing inside Burma with a load of trouble for the Japanese.

Bullocks played their part in the war against the Japanese. They were being flown from India and were trained to carry heavy loads on their backs. This one was about to make its first contact with Burmese soil after its flight from India.

River bathing made for a change and relaxation after coming off duty. Some of the anti-aircraft gunners are here seen having a dip near an airfield in Burma.

Medical orderlies about to lift a wounded man from the plane which had flown him back to India. The bamboo poles were used to pen the mules which the plane carried on the 'in' flight. The patient is Sapper F Underwood of Driffield, Yorkshire.

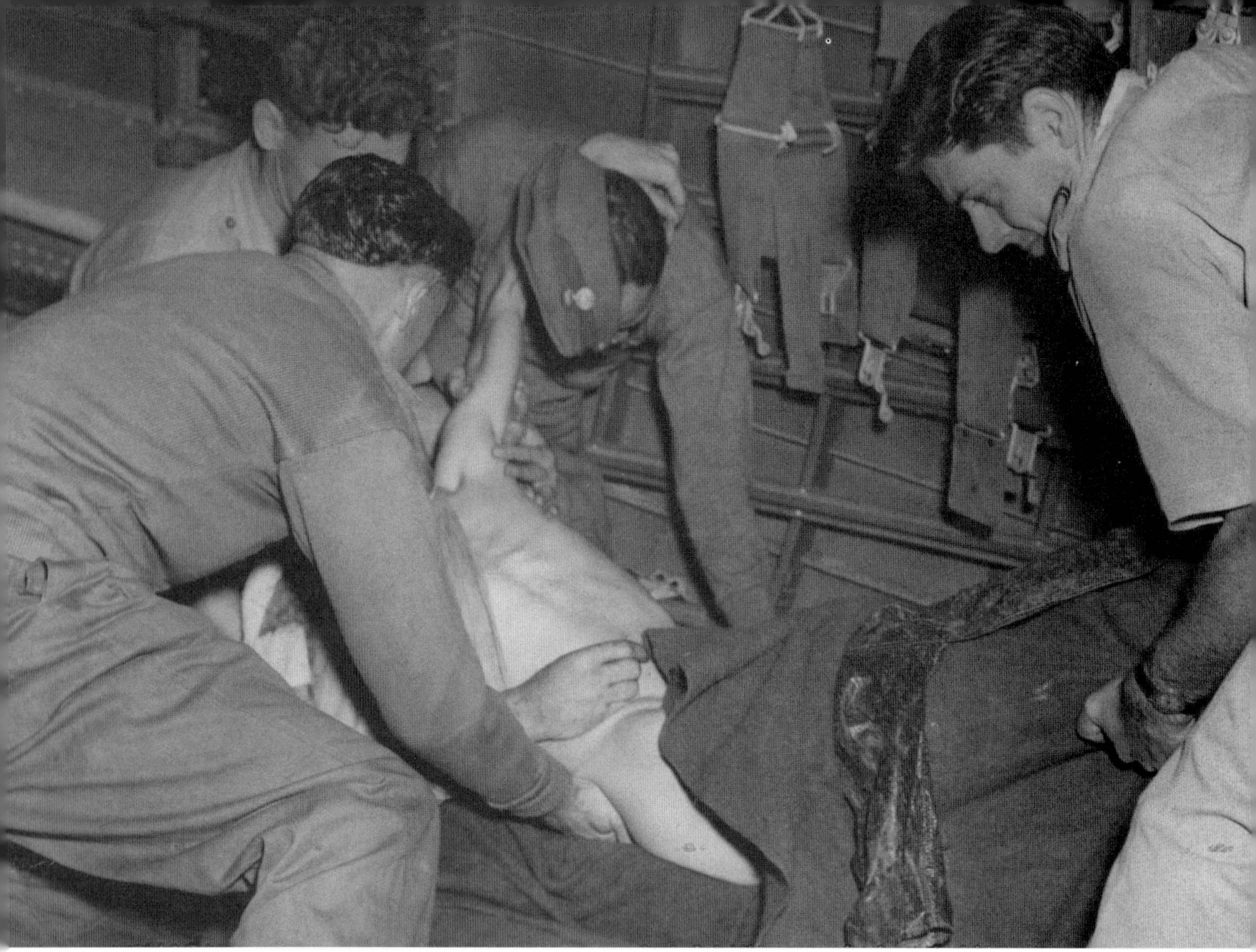

Arrived in India a wounded man is carefully lifted onto a stretcher before going into the waiting ambulance.

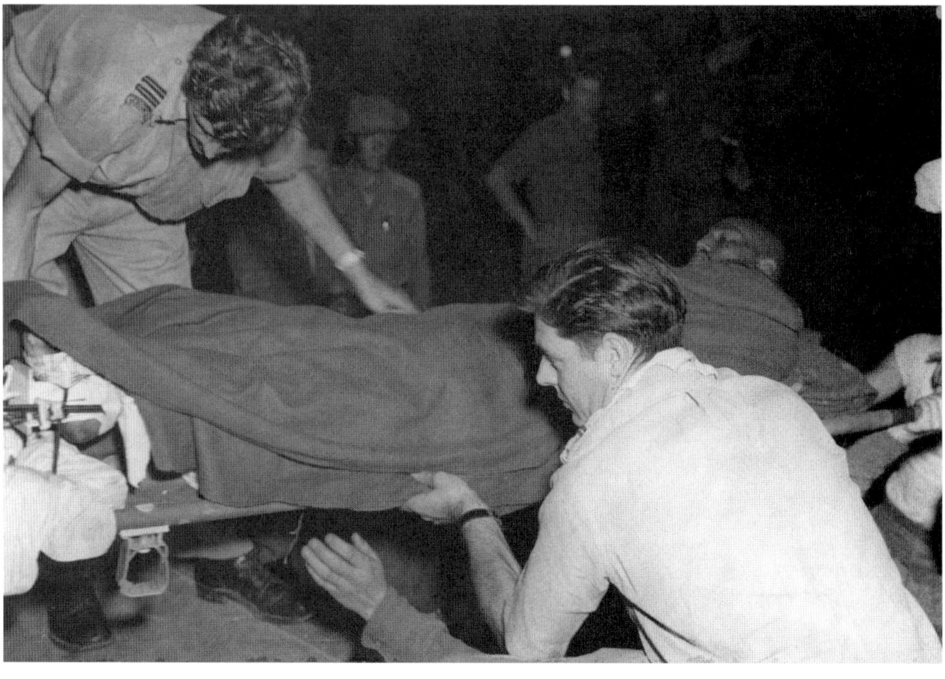

Members of the crew helping lift a wounded Gurkha from an evacuation plane.

A Gurkha stretcher case being lifted out of the plane on arrival in India while another waits his turn.

Indian troops leaving an American aircraft.

Not a wild west rodeo act but a mule reluctant to de-plane.

This mule was glad to arrive.

Men of a Leicestershire regiment awaiting zero hour before they take off for Burma by air in an RAF Dakota from 194 Squadron.

West African troops boarding an aircraft which will carry them deep into the heart of Burma to join the many thousands of British troops already there.

Pilots and crew of supply aircraft, which have just brought casualties of the Wingate Expedition back to India, having a hearty meal in a forward area.

ORDE WINGATE

Right and opposite: The architect of the two Chindit expeditions had been the recently-promoted Major General Orde Wingate DSO & 2 Bars. On 24 March 1944, as the second expedition was in full operation, Wingate flew to check three Chindit-held bases. On the return flight his B-25 Mitchell crashed into the jungle near the village of Thiulon in Manipur, India killing Wingate and the nine men on board the aircraft with him. There were stories of a damaged aircraft and also of sabotage but the one certainty is that the crash killed one of the most innovative, if eccentric, allied leaders of the Second World War.